Just Like Mike

Written by Marsha McKenzie

Illustrated by Cristal Baldwin

PROLOGUE

My main goal for this book is to help parents and teachers educate students about the challenges and joys of having a child with cerebral palsy in their classroom. I first met Michael Taylor when he came to Governor's Ranch Elementary School in Littleton, Colorado, as a third grader. At the time, I was a sixth grade teacher at the school and will never forget meeting Michael and beginning what would become a lifelong friendship with this fine young man.

From the beginning, Michael's contagious smile and outgoing personality stole the hearts of all who met him. I was fortunate to have Michael in my class when he entered sixth grade and saw for myself the positive impact he had on those around him. Although his cerebral palsy is a disability which brought with it many difficulties and challenges, his focus was always on learning, playing, working, and being positive every day. The teachers at Governor's Ranch worked to encourage students to think of Michael as "differently abled" vs. disabled. This was made easier by the fact that Michael never sought out special treatment and did his best to fit in with the other students.

Over time, his classmates came to understand that although he was different, Michael was "cool." By adopting Michael's perspective, they found themselves focusing on the things they had in common vs. the ways in which they were different. Over the years, Michael's courage, determination, and positive attitude made him a role model to his classmates, family, and teachers. Hence the title of this book, JUST LIKE MIKE.

The bonds of friendship that Michael made in elementary school continued through middle school, high school, and into adulthood. He graduated from Columbine High School in 2013 and continues to live and work in Littleton, surrounded by friends and family who love him.

I owe a sincere debt of gratitude to the many family and friends who encouraged me to write this book! To my husband, Patrick, for suggesting that I write my first children's book about Michael. To my daughters, Katie and Mallory, for cheering me on to become a writer in the first place. To all my friends and teaching colleagues for providing the support and input that got this project off the ground: Conner Dorris, Maddie Griffin, Kelly Kershisnik, Debbie Kotas, Sue Miller, and Brady and Lori Young. Finally, but most importantly, thank you, Michael, for being my collaborator, my inspiration, and my friend.

Marsha McKenzie
Michael's 6th Grade Teacher

Do you have a classmate or friend who has cerebral palsy?

Cerebral palsy is when your brain and muscles don't communicate.

Students with cerebral palsy can still learn like other people can learn, even though they move and talk differently than you.

Mike can do most things like line up for school and follow the rules ... just like you.

Mike does the best he can at school,
just like the rest of the students do.

In the classroom, he loves to hang out in the reading nook and look at his favorite books.

You don't have to guess that Mike always says yes to recess.

Mike loves sports. His family and friends take him to see the local baseball, football, basketball and hockey games.

Mike is an adult now and does a good job where he works at the movie theater.

Mike likes sports, science fiction and animation movies. His favorite movie is about a football player who never gives up on his dream.

Mike loves to travel. He would like to visit Ireland. When he was in fifth grade, he went to Washington, D.C. He got to meet the president.

So remember to include your friends
or classmates in all activities, whether
they're like you or **just like Mike.**

To Michael Taylor
With best wishes,

About the Author

Marsha McKenzie worked in the education field for 25 years. She taught at Governor's Ranch Elementary in Littleton, Colorado, for 11 years. She currently lives in Colorado Springs, Colorado, with her husband, Patrick, and their two cats, Beau and Ruby.

About the Illustrator

Cristal Baldwin lives in the small town of London, Ohio, with her husband, son Wyatt, a rescue dog, kitty, and another rescue cat. For inspiration before she begins drawing, the artist shares scripts with her insightful 7-year-old son whose feedback is always refreshingly honest. She received her fine arts degree from Wittenberg University, in Springfield, Ohio, and continues to create a variety of artwork through Flying Frog Studio.

CPSIA information can be obtained
at www.ICGtesting.com
Printed in the USA
LVHW071613100721
692202LV00016B/181